Super-Simple creative costumes

Sue Astroth

• mix & match your way to make believe •

C&T PUBLISHING

Text © 2007 Sue Astroth

Artwork © 2007 C&T Publishing, Inc.

Publisher: Amy Marson

Editorial Director: Gailen Runge

Acquisitions Editor: Jan Grigsby

Editor: Stacy Chamness

Technical Editors: Helen Frost, Gayl Gallagher

Cover Designer: Kristy K. Zacharias

Design Director/Book Designer: Kristy K. Zacharias

Junior Designer: Kiera Lofgreen

Production Coordinators: Kiera Lofgreen, Kirstie L. Pettersen

Illustrator: Kirstie L. Pettersen

Copyeditor: Cynthia Keyes Hilton

Proofreader: Wordfirm Inc.

Photography: C&T Publishing, Inc., unless otherwise noted

Published by C&T Publishing, Inc., P.O. Box 1456, Lafayette, CA 94549

Library of Congress Cataloging-in-Publication Data
Astroth, Sue,
  Super-simple creative costumes : mix & match your way to make believe /
Sue Astroth.
    p. cm.
  ISBN-13: 978-1-57120-361-8 (paper trade : alk. paper)
  ISBN-10: 1-57120-361-3 (paper trade : alk. paper)
  1. Costume. I. Title.
  TT633.A87 2006
  646.4'78—dc22
2006018272

Printed in China

10 9 8 7 6 5 4 3 2 1

Acknowledgments

This book would not have come together without the talented people at C&T Publishing and Stampers Warehouse.

THANK YOU TO:

Stacy Chamness—for your editing and your fabulous pattern-drawing ability. The shoes and frog feet are awesome!

Helen Frost—for your fantastic way of interpreting my drawings into patterns and instructions

Jan Grigsby—for your talents with tulle and a glue gun

Teresa Stroin—for your awesome satin stitching

Lynn Koolish—for an unbelievable and amazing tutti-frutti hat

Sara MacFarland—for your wonderful pet-collar creations, not to mention lunch!

Gailen Runge—for coming up with this book idea in the first place and the beautiful palette, brush, and photo album

Carolyn Aune—for your charming little ladybug

Liz Aneloski—for the delightful flower

Phyllis Nelson—for your continuous support, words of wisdom, and friendship

Terrece Siddoway—for the truly inspired elephant ears and trunk, and knitting bag

Vanessa Cole—for your friendship and creative support

Krista Camacho—for your ab fab realistic playing card creation and providing inspiration for the hula costumes

Allison Halligan—for your wonderful embellishment work

Debby Debenedetti—for just being Debby

Gary Debenedetti—for providing technical and carpentry support on Cupid's bow

My family—who are constantly surrounded by fabrics, supplies, and various tools for my creations and who are indirectly affected by my deadlines and various artistic moods—I thank you for loving me in spite of all this!

. . . and to Jois—you make it fun—still!

This book is for everyone

contents

who still believes in make believe.

ideas & insp

Creative combinations that make for super-simple costumes!

NURSE: *Pets can wear costumes, too! Nurse Cap, Bag and Accessories on pages 57–58*

VAMPIRE: *Capes on page 49; Medallions on page 50*

SUPERHERO: *Wrist wear on page 41, use a matching Badge (page 45) as a belt buckle*

iration

PRINCESS BRIDE: *Crowns on page 24, pre-made princess dress*

CLOWN: *Top Hat on page 28; Clown Tie on page 35; Pail on page 43; Silly Shoes on page 40*

PIRATE: *Headband Hat, Eyepatch, Sash on pages 54–55; Spyglass on page 43*

HULA GIRL AND LITTLE HULA GIRL: *Hula Skirts, Leis, Hairclip on pages 59–61; wristbands on page 41*

A variation on the Silly Shoes from page 40

QUEEN'S KNIGHT: *Crowns on page 24; Sword and Shield on pages 65–66*

By using a bit of faux fur and varying the Silly Shoes pattern (on the pullout), you can make paws. Rowr!

CUPID *on pages 62-64*

HALLOWEEN WAITRESS: *Crowns on page 24; Pails on page 43; Bugs on page 69*

DEVIL: *Capes on page 49; Headband Hats on page 23; Pitchfork on page 33*

Sew some fast2fuse creations on your pet's collar for a special occasion!

creative costuming

My parents loved to make special presents for me. I remember lots of doll clothes, a pretty pink basket made into a doll bed (complete with matching linens and nightgown), even a cool two-story dollhouse that had its own hand-operated elevator! One year for Christmas, Mom and Dad made me a trunk filled with wonderful dress-up clothes and jewelry. I was in heaven!

My friends and I played with those dress-up clothes for hours. One minute we would be kings and queens, the next we would pretend we were at a diner . . . we could play dress-up forever, changing themes as fast as we could change our costumes.

Kids of all ages like to wear costumes. It's a great way for little ones to learn as they play, and even grown-ups like to become someone else for a while. Isn't it fun to see adults in costume driving down the road on Halloween?

With all these things in mind, these fast2fuse costumes were created for you. A number of full costumes and costume pieces that will work for young and old kids alike are included. With just some fabric, fast2fuse, hook-and-loop tape, and a little elastic, you can create a fun and exciting costume to match your personality.

That's me in the chicken mask . . . I thought the mask was the perfect finishing touch for a princess costume.

Where to Get Ideas

Ideas for costumes can come from any number of places: magazines, books, television, movies . . . even a favorite hobby can inspire a unique costume.

What You'll Need

First, let's review some of the basic tools and supplies you'll want to have available when you start your costume projects.

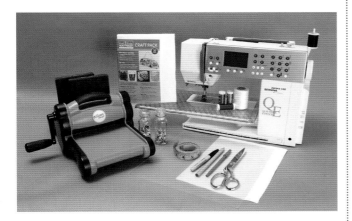

Tools

SEWING MACHINE

A sewing machine is a must for these projects. Make sure it is in good working order and has (at minimum) a basic straight and zigzag stitch. If you have to borrow a machine or you aren't familiar with yours, spend a little time getting to know how your machine operates before you start your project. Oil your machine according to the manufacturer's directions. Clean out any lint from the bobbin area and under the throat plate with a brush. Now, play a little—stitch length and width, wind a bobbin, change a needle—all the things you may want or need to do when you're in the middle of making your costume. It's also very important to know how to adjust the tension on your sewing machine. Tension is the tightness of both the spool and bobbin threads. Each type of material or thread you use will require a slightly different tension to keep your seams even and your stitches neat. Knowing how to use your machine before you start working on your costume will both save you precious sewing time and cut down on your frustration!

As a precaution and to ensure my machine is in good working order, I try to take it to the shop where I purchased it once a year for a tune-up. This way, I'm ready to start sewing at any time.

All the costumes in the book were made with a size 12 to size 14 topstitching sewing machine needle. I have found that these needles allow me to sew with almost any combination of fabric and thread with ease.

If your machine is computerized or has lots of fancy stitch capabilities, you can add all sorts of embellishments to your costumes. Consider stitching a name on your waitress costume to continue the theme, or add lots of fancy stitches on your butterfly or dragonfly wings. What a fun way to add embellishment without using more than your machine and some thread!

CUTTING TOOLS & MATS

While I use both scissors and rotary cutters, for the costumes I did find myself pulling out the fabric scissors a bit more often when cutting out specific shapes and smaller pattern pieces. During an average sewing project, my scissors take a backseat to the speed and accuracy of the 60mm rotary cutter, combined with a straight-edge ruler and self-healing cutting mat.

For some of the smaller basic shapes, I was able to use my die-cutting machine. This is a tool that has been made popular in the scrapbook and paper arts world. It allows you to cut out various shapes using set patterns or dies, from a variety of materials, making it great for little extras for all of your costumes!

The stars and flowers and the bases for these fairy wands were all cut with my die-cut machine.

MEASURING DEVICES

My favorites are:

12˝, 24˝, and 36˝ see-through rulers The markings are clear, allowing me to cut small or large pieces of fabric and fast2fuse; I can cut with the fabric grain or use the angle feature and cut on the bias.

12˝ square see-through ruler This allows me to even up pattern pieces.

Self-healing cutting mat This tool, in conjunction with a see-through ruler, allows me to make straight cuts and measure out larger pieces of cloth. The one-inch grid marks on the mat come in very handy.

Measuring tape I still like to have these handy. They are good for measuring out yardage, trims, elastic, and hook-and-loop tape.

PATTERN PAPER, INTERFACING, AND MARKING TOOLS

I typically use just about anything that's handy when I'm making a pattern. Large 24˝ × 36˝ sheets of paper are great for creating accessory patterns and can be taped together for the larger costume pieces. If I want larger pieces without the extra work, I prefer middle- to heavyweight interfacing, or actual pattern paper. Both are available at your local fabric store in the interfacing section. Newspaper is another great, inexpensive source for pattern paper.

I use a pencil for creating paper patterns, a permanent marker for plastic patterns or templates, and a ballpoint pen on plain fast2fuse. I prefer chalk markers on prepared fast2fuse (fast2fuse with fabric fused to each side). It's good to have white, yellow, and pink chalk available so you are ready for either light or dark fabrics.

When drawing or creating a pattern piece with a pencil, I will go over the piece several times until I get the exact shape I want. Once I'm happy with the results, I draw around the final pattern lines with a permanent marker.

Since most of the costume patterns are symmetrical, only one half or one quarter of the pattern is shown. Trace the partial pattern, then flip or pivot the pattern paper to trace the rest. Make a full pattern before tracing it to the fast2fuse.

Cutting diagrams are given for costume pieces with mostly straight edges. Measure and mark the pattern paper according to the diagram. Use a ruler to draw lines between the marks. Cut out the pattern on the interior lines and trace onto the fast2fuse.

 Remember to cut inside the marked lines, so the lines do not end up in your finished project.

Once I have a pattern piece drawn, I sometimes use a copier to copy the pattern onto cardstock. Cardstock's thickness gives a template more durability, especially if you are going to use the piece over and over again. The copier also provides the flexibility to reduce or enlarge the design with minimal effort. If a copier isn't available, just draw the template pattern onto cardstock.

Plastic lids work well to create templates for smaller items that need to be traced again and again.

fancy-fabric tips

○ Use sewing machine needles that match the fabric type.

○ Set your iron according to the fabric content and use a pressing cloth so you don't burn or melt the fabric.

○ Adjust the tension on your sewing machine to ensure smooth stitching on the different materials.

Don't let these suggestions turn you away from the fun fabrics; these precautions will provide you with a more pleasurable sewing experience.

FABRIC

My favorites are the Tonga batiks by Timeless Treasures. The solids are more of a tone-on-tone blend that adds just a little extra to your costume.

Walking into a fabric store, you'll find all sorts of fabrics just waiting to be made into wonderful things. Now comes the hardest part—selecting which fabric(s) to use in your costume. Your choice will depend on several things, such as how much money you want to spend, how much time you have to make the costume, and how elaborate you want the embellishments.

For many of the costumes included in the book, a good, basic solid or near-solid cotton fabric would be a great choice. It's easy to work with, easy to wear, and usually less expensive than patterned fabric. Plus, with so many colors available, it should be easy to find just the right color or combination of colors for your costume.

I also like to mix in some fun, bright novelty patterns. In the end, though, it is the vision in my head that directs my fabric purchases.

tip *I'm usually too eager to get started to wash the fabric before I begin to sew. I would slow down a bit and wash it if I felt it had too much sizing in it or was a very intense color that might run, or ruin other fabrics it touches.*

For a few of the costumes and some of the embellishments, you may want to try some of the specialty fabrics—tulle, lamé, satin, or nylon. They add such a wonderful touch of sparkle or realism to your outfit. Just take a little extra care when sewing on these fancy fabrics.

edging options

For most of the costumes in the book, I chose to satin stitch around the edges to finish them. Don't want to finish edges with satin stitching? No problem! Here are some other options:

LOOSE ZIGZAG OR STRAIGHT STITCHING Holds the layers together for a quick costume.

PREPACKAGED BIAS BINDING May be a bit tricky around some tight corners, but just follow the manufacturer's instructions.

PAINTING Some paints will soak right into your fabric; others, like puff paint, will sit right on the surface. Test your paint on a scrap of prepared fast2fuse to make sure you get the look you like.

LEAVE 'EM PLAIN Just make sure to iron around the edges of your costume pieces to be sure they are securely fused together. We used this method on the *Palette* and *Paintbrush* edges (page 22).

THREAD

I typically used all-cotton thread or a good-quality poly/cotton blend for most of the projects in the book. I generally try to match the thread color to my fabric as closely as possible, which may even lead me to a 100% polyester thread for the sake of design. If there isn't a true match, I try to go a shade slightly darker—it is more pleasing to my eye. If you like to shake things up, you may want to go with a high-contrast color for that added pizzazz on your finished piece. Satin stitching can take lots of thread, depending on how dense you like the stitches. When you purchase your fabric, make sure to buy enough spools of thread for your project.

For smaller items, such as accessories, I buy two or three spools. For full costumes I buy five or six spools. I usually try to get one more spool than I think I'll need because I really dislike running out in the middle of a project. Most stores are good about exchanging unused spools of thread for a color that will match your next project.

These costumes are great for trying out some of those specialty threads you see in fabric stores. If you have been anxious to try some of the beautiful variegated or metallic threads, you now have a great opportunity—let your imagination have some fun and play a little.

FAST2FUSE

This is the base for all the costumes and most of the accessories in the book. It is an interfacing that is fusible on both sides. Found in most fabric and quilting shops in the pattern or interfacing area, fast2fuse is 28″ wide and is usually available by the bolt, by the yard, or in 14″ × 18″ pre-cut craft packs. It is available in both lightweight and heavyweight versions, depending on the degree of firmness you need. If the weight of the fast2fuse is not listed for a project, either weight will work.

Flexible fast2fuse can be sewn, painted, covered with fabric, and cut into various shapes and sizes. For most of the smaller and medium-sized projects in the book, I fused a piece of my selected fabric to a large piece of fast2fuse, then cut out the shape I needed.

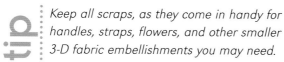 *Keep all scraps, as they come in handy for handles, straps, flowers, and other smaller 3-D fabric embellishments you may need.*

A more economical way to use the fast2fuse for larger pieces is to cut out your desired shape from the fast2fuse, then fuse that piece to the wrong side of the fabric. Cut out the shape, then fuse it to the wrong side of a second piece of fabric. Trim, then finish the edges as you desire. For the large costumes, only the outside of the fast2fuse is covered with fabric.

tip *If you prefer to completely cover all of the fast2fuse on the inside of a costume, here are a few options:*

- *Cover it with the same fabric as the outside of the costume. Be sure to double the listed fabric amounts.*
- *Use a less expensive cut of fabric or muslin.*
- *Paint the inside!*

NOTE: In the instructions throughout the book, I call fast2fuse with fabric fused to each side **prepared fast2fuse**. Even if only one side of the piece will show, having fabric on both sides makes a better finished edge. I will list a certain color of fabric if the color is important for the theme of the costume.

tip *If you prepare a lot of fast2fuse for cutting into various shapes and you try to use every inch possible, you might run into a piece with one side not completely covered with fabric. One way to fix this is to cut a length of the selvage edge from the same piece of fabric, long enough to cover the exposed fast2fuse and wide enough so the selvage of the fabric overlaps the previously fused fabric. Overlap the selvage about ¼″, fuse it, and trim away the excess. You can now continue with your project.*

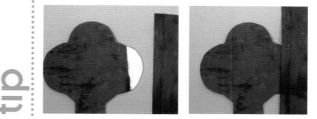

Sewing Your Costumes

For a finished look, I chose to stitch around the edges of the prepared fast2fuse with a wide satin stitch. Experiment with the length and width to get a stitch you prefer. Overlap the stitching at corners and points. When satin stitching, don't backstitch at the end; tie off the threads instead. Then either trim the ends or thread them through a large tapestry needle and make a stitch under the previous stitching to hide them. At the beginning and ending of straight-stitched seams, always backstitch.

When stitching costume pieces together, I try to sew the wrong sides together, just to the inside of the satin stitching.

Costume Closures

I use a variety of closures and ties for the various pieces and parts of each costume. I probably use sew-on hook-and-loop tape the most. Hook-and-loop tape offers a secure closing for the *Hula Girl Lei* (page 59). Not only could I hide my stitching behind the flowers, but the tape enables the piece to fit different-sized people.

Ribbon is another closure that can be functional as well as adding another decorative embellishment. For the *Little Hula Girl Lei* (page 61), I sewed lengths of ribbon to each end, making for easy tying and the ability to fit a variety of sizes.

I also like to use fabric for costume shoulder straps. I use the same fabric as on the main parts of the costume and create finished strips about 22½″ long and 2½″ wide. I sew these to either side of the costume, leaving them long enough to tie a knot or bow. I used this method on the *Playing Card* costume (page 19). For the *Knitting Bag* costume (page 18), Terrece used bias tape as a ready-to-use alternative to fabric straps.

tip

To create finished straps, start with a 4″ to 6″-wide strip cut from the width of the fabric. Fold in half lengthwise with right sides together. Sew the lengthwise edges together using a ½″ seam allowance. Turn right side out, and press with the seam in the center of one side.

additional supplies

○ **IRON AND IRONING BOARD** A must for fusing fabric to fast2fuse. A small tabletop ironing board is great when you are working on smaller pieces or embellishments.

○ **HAND-SEWING AND TAPESTRY NEEDLES** For sewing buttons, fibers, and other various embellishments when you don't want to use glue.

○ **SHANK REMOVER** This tool lets you remove the shank of a button. Great for times you'd prefer to glue instead of sew.

○ **WIRE CUTTERS** While it's possible to cut some lightweight wire with your craft scissors, an inexpensive pair of wire cutters to cut the wire used in a couple of the patterns will save your scissors!

○ **GLUE** A good fabric and/or tacky glue that dries clear. I like The Ultimate! and Fabri-Tac.

○ **GLUE GUN** I don't recommend using a glue gun for fabric, but for some of the accessories in the book it was simply the easiest way to stick everything together.

NOTE: When using a glue gun on metal embellishments, put the glue where the embellishment will be placed, then place the embellishment into the glue. Otherwise, the embellishment may get too hot to handle and burn your fingers. If you prefer to put the glue directly on the metal embellishment, use tweezers or pliers to hold it while adding glue.

○ **AWL** Good for making holes in prepared fast2fuse when applying brads.

○ **SCREW PUNCH** This tool, with various-size bits, is extremely helpful when making holes for brads.

○ **HOOK-AND-LOOP TAPE** Comes in colors to match or blend with just about any costume. I prefer the sew-on variety, as the glue from the stick-on type tends to gum up sewing machine needles.

Embellishing Your Costumes

tape (which can be painted and/or stenciled), or for wider strips try cutting up old or inexpensive sheets.

Don't forget to check out your local thrift store for a variety of embellishments, from buttons off clothing to yarns, ribbons, and other fun items that just might do the trick!

The beading section of your favorite craft store, or maybe your jewelry box, can provide you with some wonderful embellishment options. I found these "jewels" at my local sewing store. I cut some diamonds out of cardstock and painted them gold, sewed them in place, and simply glued the jewels to the cardstock.

Once the basic costume is constructed, the real fun begins—embellishing! With costumes, it's not necessarily just adding stuff to the costume; it's defining and refining the persona you want your costume to have—cute or scary, whimsical or realistic.

Many of the costume embellishments are created with more fabric and thread, such as the paint of the *Palette* and *Paintbrush* (page 22) and the red cross on the *Nurse's Cap* (page 57). I fused HeatnBond Lite to fabric and made fabric patches for the paint blobs and red cross. Then I simply ironed them where I wanted them, and did a decorative stitch around the edges. It's easy to do, and the supplies are readily available at your local fabric store.

Paint is a good way to add detail to a flat surface. You can apply it with a foam brush, a bristle brush, or even a small roller, depending on the size of your project. There are many styles of paint to choose from, in every color under the sun.

Everything is fair game to help you create the look you want. For parts on some of the costumes, you may want to add different materials. To give the feeling of hair, a tail, or a mane, consider using twine or string, strips of fabric, ribbon, or yarn. Maybe a combination of all four would give you the look you want. Sometime you'll want to add ribbon for some decoration. Check out the ribbon section at your local fabric store, or make some yourself from strips cut from fabric or duct

I love the look of beading around the edges of some of the costume accessories, but I don't have the time or desire to stitch all the beads by hand. One day, while pinning some fabric together, I noticed that the tops of the pins I was using looked just like beads. They come in a variety of colors and you can find them on the notions wall at your local fabric or variety store. I think they are perfect edge embellishments on costume accessories!

NOTE: Be careful if you are using the pins on something for a child of any age. Make sure to glue them in place so they don't fall out and hurt someone.

Embellishments are all the rage for those who love to scrapbook life's memories, and the scrapbook companies are doing their best to keep up with the demand. Many of the 3-D treasures translate to various other crafts, including embellishing costumes. The variety is amazing: you can find something for just about every style of costume. Check out your local store to see what you can find—I'm sure you will be amazed.

Glitter is another way to transform an ordinary costume into a *wow*! It is an inexpensive way to add glamour and sparkle to an item. Scrapbook stores carry an extensive color selection. Add glitter with either fabric glue from the glitter company or good quality tacky glue. When you want glitter to cover a large area, just paint on the glue with a paintbrush—no dilution necessary. Place the piece in a tray or on a large piece of waxed paper, and sprinkle the glitter over the wet glue. Let this dry, shake the loose glitter back into the tray, and then determine whether you need to add more or fill in any gaps.

You can find embellishments everywhere. It's all in the way you look at what an item *can be*, versus what an item *is*. My friend Vanessa works in the receiving area of a scrapbook store. She is always asking me if I want various plastic corners, cardboard tubes, or other packaging materials for my projects.

Measurements

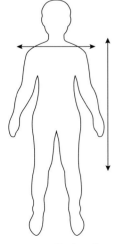

I tried to keep this pretty easy. Most costumes in the book will fit kids up to adult. The shapes are simple and with a small amount of alteration, adding an inch or so or cutting off an inch all the way around the pattern, you can adjust them to the size you need. You may even be able to use the enlarging feature on your home printer or copy machine. I focused on some pretty basic measurements for the full costume construction, measuring from the neck down to the knees, and from one shoulder to the other—and

adjusted project measurements as necessary. I also included front-to-back measurements for the around-the-body costumes. As with just about any pattern you make, it's a really good idea to make a paper pattern first to ensure that you get the proper size.

costume safety

The most important thing to remember when creating a costume is to have fun! The very next most important thing is to make sure the costume will be safe for you or your loved ones to wear. Here are some safety suggestions to consider . . . they are pretty basic, but better safe than sorry!

○ Don't make the costume so big that it becomes difficult to walk in. Also consider whether you will be sitting or not . . . maybe, instead of a full costume, you only need a single front piece.

○ If you're going trick-or-treating, make sure you are visible to people and cars. Try to add some reflective tape to your costume—or even your shoes—so people and cars can see you.

○ Make sure your line of sight is clear.

○ Don't make anything too tight around your neck.

○ Don't use glitter on glasses—it can easily flake off and could harm your eyes.

Costume Combinations

In the book we have a number of full costumes as well as accessories that are great additions to a costume or make fun dress-up toys, or might even make good gifts for your friends. Many of the costumes in the book come in pieces—you can select various pieces and come up with a great unique costume. They require a basic wardrobe of tights and a leotard, plain sweats, or a simple shirt and pants. As your costume develops, you may want to add to these basics . . . but if you don't have much time, the basics will always get you through.

Now, let's start playing make-believe!

scrapbook

The book is simply a box shape with an extra piece in front for the book cover!

what you'll need

- 5 yards of heavyweight fast2fuse
- 1¾ yards of red fabric
- 1¾ yards of cream fabric
- 8 yards of ½"-wide fusible web
- 1¾ yards of 1"-wide black ribbon
- 6 yards of 1"-wide gold ribbon

How-Tos

1. Cut 6 pieces 22" × 28" and 4 pieces 10" × 28" of fast2fuse.

2. Stack and sew the fast2fuse pieces together in matched-size pairs. Use straight stitching around the outside to create a double thickness of the fast2fuse.

3. Cut 1 piece 32" × 58" from the red fabric and 1 piece 32" × 56" from the cream fabric.

4. Place a 22"-wide fast2fuse pair on the end of the red fabric, 2" in from the end and the sides. Fuse in place.

5. Position a 10"-wide fast2fuse pair next to the first piece and fuse. Repeat with another 22" pair and fuse, leaving about 6" of the long edge unfused.

6. Place a 10"-wide fast2fuse pair on the end of the cream fabric, 2" in from the end and sides. Fuse in place.

7. Position a 22"-wide fast2fuse pair next to the first and fuse in place.

8. Place the red fabric piece face down with the unfused end to the right. Place the cream fabric piece on top, fabric side up, and with the unfused fabric to the left.

9. Fuse the cream fabric to the fast2fuse. The end of the fabric is even with the fast2fuse. This piece is the front cover of the book.

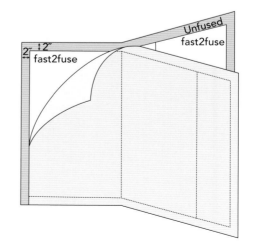

10. To form the box shape, wrap the other end of the cream fabric to the back and fuse in place. Fold the unfused edge of the red fabric under so the crease is even with the edge of the fast2fuse. Use a fusible web strip to fuse the red fabric to the cream fabric.

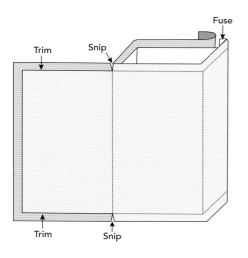

Finishing the Edges:

1. For the cover, snip the red and cream fabrics to the edge of the fast2fuse where the book cover attaches to the box of the book.

2. Trim the cream fabric even with the fast2fuse all the way around the book cover.

3. On the cover, fold the edges of the red fabric in 1″ and press. Fuse a strip of fusible web to the folded edges on all 3 sides.

4. Fold the red fabric over and fuse it to the inside of the cover.

5. To complete the top and bottom of the box, fold the fabric to the inside and fuse to the fast2fuse.

6. Try on the costume to determine the length and placement for the straps. Sew in place.

7. Use fusible web strips to add the gold ribbon to the cover or embellish as desired! You could be a scrapbook or a favorite childhood story, or try transferring actual pictures onto fabric to become a brag book.

knitting bag

This project does not have a pattern. You simply cut the pieces to fit the person who will wear your masterpiece.

what you'll need

○ 3 yards of heavyweight fast2fuse

○ 3 yards total of brown fabrics

○ Matching thread

○ 1 package of $7/8$"-wide bias tape

How-Tos

1. To determine the width of the front and back pieces: Measure the person from shoulder to shoulder and add 6".

The length will be 28", the width of the fast2fuse.

Cut out 2 pieces with the above measurements.

2. To determine the width of your sidepieces: Measure the person's side (from front to back) and add 2".

The length will be 28", the width of the fast2fuse.

Cut out 2 pieces with the above measurements.

3. Fuse the fabric to the fast2fuse. Trim the fabric so it is even with the fast2fuse.

4. Satin stitch around each piece.

5. Join the pieces by placing the wrong sides together and sewing with a straight stitch just inside the edge of the satin stitching. Sew one sidepiece to the front of the bag. Repeat for the remaining side and back pieces. Join the front/sidepiece to the back/sidepiece.

6. Following the diagram, make the pattern for the handles. Trace onto fast2fuse and cut out 2 handles. Fuse fabric to each side. Trim the fabric even with the fast2fuse.

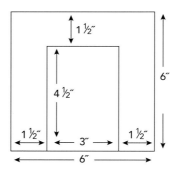

7. Satin stitch around each handle piece.

8. Sew the handles to the front and back of the bag, as shown in the photo.

9. Try on the costume to determine the length and placement for the straps. Sew in place.

10. Embellish the bag as desired.

playing card

We went very traditional, but you could easily personalize this costume with fabric and playing card selection. You could even create a sports card of your child, or an altered trading card!

what you'll need

- 1⅜ yards of heavyweight fast2fuse
- 1¼ yards of lightweight fast2fuse
- 1½ yards of white fabric
- ⅓ yard of black fabric
- ¾ yard of print fabric
- Matching thread
- Hot glue gun

How-Tos

1. Cut 2 pieces 22″ × 28″ of heavyweight fast2fuse and 1 piece 18″ × 24″ of lightweight fast2fuse. Trim the corners to round them.

2. Cut three 10″ circles and 1 piece 10″ × 15″ of lightweight fase2fuse.

3. Fuse the white fabric to the heavyweight fast2fuse pieces. Trim the fabric even with the fast2fuse.

4. Fuse the print fabric to the 18″ × 24″ piece of fast2fuse and the 10″ circles. Trim the fabric.

5. Enlarge the spade pattern 200% for the center of the card. Use your computer to create the number or letter of your choice. Print in the largest size of font and enlarge if necessary to measure 4″ high.

6. Fuse the black fabric to the 10″ × 15″ piece of fast2fuse. Cut out the card's suit and numbers or letters.

7. Satin stitch around each piece.

8. Glue the card suit pieces in place using the photo as a guide. Center and glue the print fabric piece and the circles to the card back.

9. Cut 1 strip 4½″ wide × the width of the white fabric. Fold the strip in half lengthwise and sew using a ½″ seam. Turn right side out and press with the seam in the center. Cut the strip in half to make 2 straps.

10. Try on the costume to determine the length and placement of the straps. Sew in place.

I didn't add any straps on the side, keeping it easy to get on and off, but you could add them if you prefer.

ladybug

Who wouldn't want this cutie to come visiting the house or garden?

what you'll need

- 2 yards of heavyweight fast2fuse
- 2 yards of red fabric
- 1¾ yards of black fabric
- Matching thread
- ½ yard of fusible web
- Assorted trims, rickrack, and ribbons to decorate front of costume

How-Tos

1. Trace the patterns from the pullout onto pattern paper. Trace onto the fast2fuse. Use the wing pattern for the body by rounding off the bottom edge. Cut the pieces out.

2. Fuse the red fabric to each side of the wing piece and the black fabric to the outside of the body and wedge pieces. Trim the edges even with the fast2fuse.

3. Satin stitch around each piece.

4. Add fusible web to the black fabric and cut 9 or 10 circles, approximately 4″ in diameter. Arrange and fuse to the wings.

5. Using your glue gun or by sewing in place, add the black wedge behind the red wings.

6. Cut 3 strips 3″ wide × the width of the black fabric. Fold the strips in half lengthwise and sew using ½″ seams. Turn right side out and press with the seam in the center. Cut into pieces approximately 14″ long to make 8 straps.

7. Sew side straps to the inside of the wing and body pieces, approximately 4½″ from the side and 15½″ from the top of the shoulder.

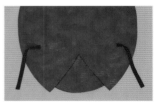

8. Sew shoulder straps to the inside of the wing and body pieces, approximately 3″ from the top and 5″ from the side. (I stitched through all layers so they could hold the costume's weight.)

9. To hold the pieces together and create a rounded look, measure 4″ down from the shoulder on each side and sew with a wide zigzag stitch for approximately 1″.

10. Using trims and ribbons and the photo as your guide, decorate the front of the costume as desired.

flower

I have provided instructions for a medium-size costume. Simply enlarge each circle measurement for a larger flower, or reduce for a smaller flower.

what you'll need

- 2 yards of heavyweight fast2fuse
- 2½ yards of dark pink fabric
- ½ yard of light pink fabric
- ¼ yard of yellow fabric
- ½ yard of green fabric
- ¼ yard of pale pink fabric
- Matching thread
- 7 Styrofoam 2″ balls
- Yellow floral spray paint (oher types will melt the Styrofoam)
- Hot glue gun
- Styrofoam glue—a must! (Hot glue will melt the Styrofoam.)

How-Tos

1. Trace the patterns from the pullout onto pattern paper. Trace 2 large flowers, 1 smaller flower, and 3 leaves onto fast2fuse and cut out.

2. Fuse the fabrics to one side of the fast2fuse, trim the excess fabric, and repeat for the other side.

3. Set aside 1 large flower for the back of the costume. Transfer the dart pattern to each petal on the other flowers. Make the darts by cutting the wedge out. Pull the edges tightly together while sewing with a wide satin stitch.

4. Satin stitch around each piece.

5. Cut a 7″ circle from the yellow fabric. Cut a 6″ circle from the fast2fuse. Center and fuse together. Clip the edges of the fabric every ½″ to create a fringe.

6. Cut the Styrofoam balls in half (a serrated knife makes this task easy). Spray paint the Styrofoam half circles. (I did this task outdoors in a shallow box to prevent any overspray.) Glue the half circles to the yellow center.

7. Refer to the photo to arrange the petals. Glue the flower layers in place.

8. Satin stitch veins onto the leaves if desired, and glue them to the back of the front flowers.

9. Cut 1 strip 5″ wide × the width of the pale pink fabric. Fold in half lengthwise and sew using a ½″ seam. Turn right side out and press with the seam in the center. Cut in half to make 2 straps.

10. Try on the costume to determine the length and placement of the shoulder straps. Sew in place.

palette

what you'll need

- 1¼ yards of heavyweight fast2fuse
- 1 yard of cream fabric
- ¼ yard or scraps of 6 bright fabrics for paint splotches
- ⅔ yard of fusible web

How-Tos

1. Fuse the cream fabric onto one side of the fast2fuse.

2. On the reverse side of the fast2fuse, draw a palette shape (like a wide kidney bean with a hole in it) approximately 28″ wide and 40″ long. Trim around the shape.

3. Fuse the web to the bright fabrics. Trim the fabric into paint splotches about 7″ across. Cut smaller drops from the scraps. Fuse to the palette.

4. Cut 1 strip 4½″ wide × the width of the cream fabric. Fold the strip in half lengthwise and sew using a ½″ seam. Turn right side out and press with the seam in the center.

5. Try on the costume to determine the length and placement of the shoulder strap. Sew in place.

paintbrush

what you'll need

- ¼ yard of heavyweight fast2fuse
- ¼ yard each of brown and black fabric
- ⅛ yard or scrap of gray fabric

How-Tos

1. Following the diagram, make a pattern. Mark and cut the pattern from fast2fuse. Cut out the brush as 1 piece.

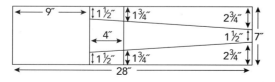

2. Fuse the black fabric to both sides of the bristle area.

3. Fuse the brown fabric to one side of the handle area.

4. Fuse the gray fabric to one side of the middle area. (I cut mine wider and turned under ¼″ along the edges first.)

5. Referring to the photo, cut the black rectangle into a bristle shape.

Optional: Fuse some bright "paint" fabric onto the bristles before trimming.

6. Fold the handle lengthwise. Sew the long edges together using a narrow zigzag stitch.

headband hats

You have so many options with this style of hat—you can be a princess, a devil, a nurse, or even a pirate!

what you'll need

- 8″ × 11″ piece of prepared fast2fuse (use a color that works with your theme)
- Matching thread
- Two ½″ buttons
- ½ yard of cord elastic
- Template material

How-Tos

1. Trace the pattern from the pullout onto template material.

2. Trace the template onto prepared fast2fuse and cut out.

3. Satin stitch around the piece.

4. Sew the buttons onto each end of the headband.

5. Make a ½″ loop at one end of the cord elastic.

6. Try on the headband, then make a loop on the other end of the cord elastic.

7. Loop the cord elastic around each button on the headband.

 Check out scrapbook stores for great embellishments that would be perfect to top off these hats!

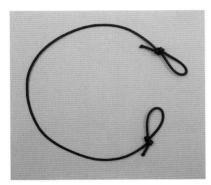

variation

Create devil horns following the pattern on the pullout

crowns

Crowns can be so much fun to play with . . . at any age! With all the fabric and embellishments to choose from, it was easy to find fun combinations for my royal headgear. Who wouldn't want to be king or queen for a day?

what you'll need

For adult size: This size fits quite a number of people, both men and women. To ensure a good fit once the pattern is drawn, measure the wearer's head and adjust if necessary.

For child size: Measure the child's head. Use the adult-size pattern and cut away 1 or 2 crown points as needed. Trim off the excess from the strips on each side.

- ○ ¼ yard of heavyweight fast2fuse
- ○ ½ yard of print fabric for adult size
- ○ ¼ yard of print fabric for child size
- ○ Matching thread
- ○ 3″ piece of hook-and-loop tape
- ○ Cardstock to decorate crown as desired
- ○ Embellishments as desired

How-Tos

1. Trace the pattern from the pullout onto pattern paper. Follow the diagram to make a pattern for the Money Man and Knight crown variations.

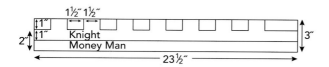

2. Fuse the fabric to both sides of the fast2fuse. Trace the pattern onto prepared fast2fuse and cut out.

3. Satin stitch around the piece.

4. Sew the hook side of the tape to the right side of the crown base. Sew the loop side of the tape to the inside of the opposite end so that when the crown is closed the hook and loop tapes will connect.

5. Embellish as desired.

You can get one child's crown out of ¼ yard, but by going up to ⅓ yard you can get two crowns if you cut carefully. Draw the crown pattern on fabric, then flip it to draw a second crown. One will have 7 points, the other will have 6. A great deal for only a few more inches of yardage!

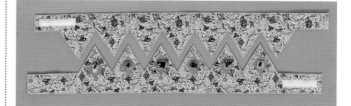

Variations

Here's one that is truly royal!

I glued a 2"-wide strip of fun fur around the bottom of the crown, making sure the fur didn't interfere with the hook-and-loop tape.

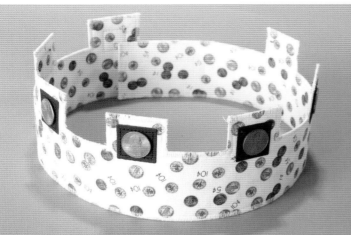

I do!

With a simple strip of lightweight fast2fuse, a little fabric glue, and some beautiful trim, you can make a lovely headpiece.

A Money Man variation for the accountant in your life.

I added wire down the center of each point so I could curl the points like a jester's hat, and then added bells for fun. Follow the instructions for adding wire to a fast2fuse project on page 35.

pointy clown hat

From clown to princess, this easy hat has lots of versatility. Once you get the basics down, you'll be ready to make more for lots of different occasions. With a change of fabrics you could easily make a wizard or sorceress hat, or use all black fabric and add a brim to it for a special little witch in your life.

what you'll need

- ½ yard of heavyweight fast2fuse
- ½ yard of black polka-dot fabric
- ⅛ yard of white fabric
- Matching thread
- White yarn or 4 pompoms
- 15″ of hook-and-loop tape
- ½ yard of ½″ elastic

How-Tos

1. Trace the pattern from the pullout onto pattern paper.

2. Overlap the straight edges 1″ and try it on to make sure the pattern fits. Adjust as necessary on the fold line of the pattern.

3. Trace the pattern onto fast2fuse and cut out.

4. Fuse the black polka-dot fabric to one side of the fast2fuse, trim the excess fabric, and repeat for the other side.

5. Satin stitch around the entire hat.

6. With the wrong side of the hat facing you, sew the loop side of the tape to the left edge. Sew the hook side of the tape to the underside on the right edge, making sure both edges will connect when the hat is wrapped together.

7. Cut 1 strip 2″ wide × the width of the white fabric. Fold a long edge under ¼″ and press. Fold ¼″ again and stitch to make a narrow hem.

NOTE: I used the selvage edge of a long piece of white fabric so I didn't have to worry about finishing the outer edge.

Stitch 2 rows of a long straight stitch along the other long edge. Pull the threads to gather the strip to fit the bottom of the hat. Stitch in place, folding about 1″ under at each end.

8. Cut a strip 1¾″ wide × the width of the black polka-dot fabric. Fold in half lengthwise and sew using a ¼″ seam. Turn right side out. Thread the elastic through to gather the fabric. Try on the hat to determine the length and placement of the chin-strap. Sew in place.

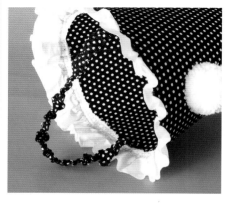

9. Make one 3″ and three 2½″ pompoms.

10. Referring to the photo, glue the larger pompom to the top of closed hat and the three smaller pompoms in a vertical row on the center front.

Variation
For your princess!

With just a change of color and lots of tulle and ribbons pouring out of the top, she is set to inherit the kingdom. To keep everything in place I sewed a curtain ring inside the top of the hat and tied the ribbons and tulle to the ring.

how to make a pompom

If you do not have a pompom tool, here is a quick way to make a simple yarn embellishment.

what you'll need

○ Skein of yarn   ○ Cardboard   ○ Scissors

How-Tos

1. Cut a strip of firm cardboard, from the back of a notepad or a box, the diameter of the pompom you need.

2. Wrap yarn around the cardboard 80–100 times. (You can do more or fewer, depending on how thick the yarn is and how full you want the pompom.)

3. Cut the end of the strand. Carefully remove the yarn from the cardboard.

4. Using an 8″ to 10″ piece of yarn, tie a *tight* and secure knot around the center of the wrapped yarn. At this point the pompom will start to fluff up.

5. Hold the yarn tails from the knot and cut the loops. Trim the pompom to the desired size.

top hat

Sometimes simple is most effective. For added embellishment, consider adding a scarf, decorating with more ribbon, or even making some fast2fuse fabric flowers to create a very special one-of-a-kind look. If you want to get really wild, add some yarn or ribbon just inside the brim to look like crazy hair!

what you'll need

- 7½″ wide × circumference of wearer's head + 1″ of striped prepared lightweight fast2fuse
- 15″ × 15″ square of polka-dot prepared lightweight fast2fuse
- 1½ yards of 1″-wide ribbon
- Matching thread

How-Tos

1. Measure the circumference of the wearer's head. Find the diameter by dividing by 3.14. Add 7″ to the diameter. Cut a circle of this diameter to form a brim of about 3″ all the way around the hat. In the center of the circle, measure and cut a circle equal to the head diameter.

2. Satin stitch around both the top and brim pieces of the hat.

3. Place the short ends of the top piece together. Sew a ½″ seam to make a cylinder. Backstitch at the beginning and end of the seam. Turn right side out and press the seam.

4. The top cylinder part of the hat should fit just inside of the inner circle on the brim. Match right sides together and carefully pin. Make any adjustments as necessary to ensure a good fit. Join the top and brim by sewing just inside the edges of the satin stitching with a straight stitch. Press the seam to the top of the hat with the tip of your iron.

5. Try on the hat and mark the placement for the ribbons. Sew ribbons in place.

tutti-frutti hat

It is amazing what a little fabric, a baseball cap, some ribbon, and some fruit can become when combined! Once you see how this one is made, you'll be thinking of other hats to make. You could also use this construction method to make one of those grand millinery creations of the Victorian era, or a larger pirate hat!

what you'll need

- 1 plain baseball cap
- 1 yard heavyweight fast2fuse
- 1⅓ yards hat fabric in color you prefer
- 2 yards of yarn trim for brim

- 2 yards of 2″-to 2½″-wide ribbon (I used a wire-edged ribbon)
- Matching thread
- Monofilament thread
- Assorted lightweight plastic fruits
- Hot glue gun

How-Tos

1. Start with a baseball cap (fit to the costume wearer's head) and remove the bill. It's best to rip out the stitching and completely remove the bill instead of cutting it off.

2. Stitch around the base of the cap to hold the layers together.

3. Draw a 22″-diameter circle for the brim pattern. Measure the diameter of the baseball cap, and draw a circle that size in the center of the 22″ circle.

4. Cut out the circles to make a doughnut-shaped pattern. Fold the pattern into quarters and mark each quarter. Using the dart pattern provided on the pullout, mark a dart on each quarter line. Cut out the darts.

5. Trace the brim pattern onto fast2fuse and cut out. Fuse the fabric to both sides. Trim the fabric even with the fast2fuse.

6. Mark and cut the darts on the brim. Sew the darts by tightly pulling the edges together and sewing with a wide satin stitch.

7. Using a wide zigzag stitch and monofilament thread, sew the trim to the brim.

8. Sew the brim to the cap with a wide satin stitch.

 tip *Sew about 5″ of satin stitching around the inside of the brim first, where the adjustable/open part of the cap will be.*

9. For the hat crown, fold the brim pattern in half and trace around it on fast2fuse. Cut it out, and wrap it around the baseball cap. Sew, glue, or fuse the edges together. Depending on the size of the hat, you may have extra that you want to cut off.

10. Wrap the fabric over the crown. Stitch or glue in place.

11. Shape the brim. I turned part of the brim up and part of it down so you can see the fruit.

12. Arrange the ribbon and fruit. Glue them in place with a hot glue gun.

deelyboppers

what you'll need

- Store-bought headband with antennae
- Four 2" hearts of prepared fast2fuse
- Matching thread
- Hot glue gun

How-Tos

1. Satin stitch around each of the hearts.

2. Remove any pre-attached decorations from the headband.

3. Using your glue gun, glue 2 hearts together, sandwiching one of the headband antennae between them. Hold until the glue cools/hardens a bit. Repeat for the second antenna.

tip *I found these headpieces at a party supply store. I simply removed the pre-attached decorations and added my own!*

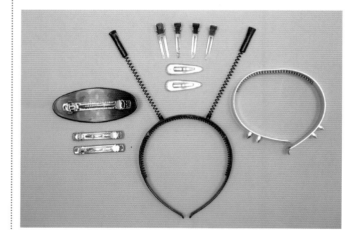

arrow head

I found this headband at an after-Halloween sale for only 50¢! It originally had a hatchet attached to the sides, but with careful removal I was set to redecorate it the way I wanted to.

what you'll need

- Headband
- 12″ × 16″ piece of prepared lightweight fast2fuse
- Matching thread
- Hot glue gun

How-Tos

1. Following the diagram, make the pattern. Trace onto prepared fast2fuse.

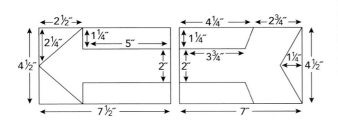

2. Cut out 2 each of both front and back arrow pieces, following the tip referring to mirror-imaged shapes on page 64.

3. Satin stitch around each of the pieces.

4. Measure and mark 2″ from the straight ends. With wrong sides together, sew the arrowheads together between the marks, leaving the ends open. Repeat for the fletchings (arrow tails).

5. Use your hot glue gun to glue the arrowhead to the headband. Wrap the back piece around the headband first, then wrap the front piece around to the back, overlapping the back piece. Repeat for the fletchings.

wands

circle wand

what you'll need

- Two 4″ circles of prepared fast2fuse
- Two 3″ circles of prepared fast2fuse
- Two 3″ flowers of prepared fast2fuse
- Matching thread
- ¼″ unfinished wood dowel
- Unfinished wood candle cup (available at a craft store or in the craft section of your local fabric store)
- Acrylic paint and foam brush
- 1⅛ yards each of 3 coordinating ribbons in widths of ¼″–⅜″
- Two 1″ buttons

How-Tos

1. Satin stitch around each piece.

2. Place the 4″ circles wrong sides together. Sew with a straight stitch just inside the edge of the satin stitching, leaving a ⅜″ to ½″ opening at the bottom.

3. Paint the dowel and candle cup. Let dry. Glue the candle cup to the end of the dowel. Seal with a varnish if desired.

tip
To help get the dowel to fit easily into the wand decoration, insert the tip of a closed pair of scissors into the opening of the sewn circles and twist.

4. With ribbons draped evenly and firmly over the top of the dowel, insert the dowel into the circles.

5. Arrange the ribbons as you desire, then remove the dowel and ribbons from the wand and add a bit of glue around the ribbons and the top. Don't add much or it will all end up at the opening of your wand.

6. Carefully slide the dowel and ribbons back into the circles. Set aside and let dry.

7. Referring to the photos, glue the remaining circles, flowers, and buttons to each side of the wand. Let dry.

Some of the various dowel caps (and a spool of thread!) I used to give the ends of the wands a finished look

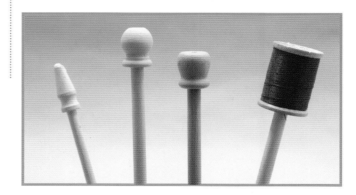

Boy, did I have fun making these (and I know you will too)!

The basic circle, heart, oval, frame, and square die cuts all lend themselves to creative wand shapes. Once I got started it was very hard to stop. I kept thinking of fun and different ideas. Don't worry if you don't have a die-cut machine. Check with your local scrapbook store to see if you can use theirs or, because the shapes are basic, just cut them out with scissors.

Variations

I used the same concept constructing the Devil's Pitchfork, but I glued it together instead of sewing it. The pattern is on the pullout.

bow tie

These ties can go from plain to fun and fancy. With a simple button and elastic closure, you can whip one up in no time.

what you'll need

- 9″ × 13″ piece of prepared lightweight fast2fuse
- Matching thread
- ¾ yard of cord elastic
- ½″ button
- Hot glue gun

How-Tos

1. Following the diagram, make a pattern. Trace onto prepared fast2fuse and cut out.

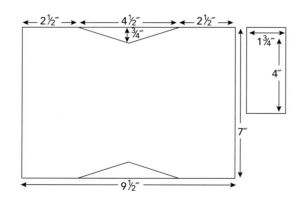

2. Satin stitch around the pieces.

3. Bunch the center of the tie together and loop the knot piece around it. Glue the knot piece in place on the back of the tie.

4. Tie a loop at one end of the cord elastic. Measure around the neck for the length and tie a button to the other end. Thread the cord elastic through the back of the knot piece. The loop goes over the button to fasten the tie.

clown tie

Adding wire to embellishments is easy and fun. You just need to be sure that the wire is sewn into the fast2fuse before you fuse the fabric and that it is placed away from your satin stitching.

what you'll need

- 6″ × 21″ piece of lightweight fast2fuse
- ¼ yard of fabric
- 33″ of 18-gauge wire
- White thread
- Matching thread
- 1¼ yards of cord elastic
- Two ⅜″ buttons

How-Tos

1. Following the diagram, make a pattern.

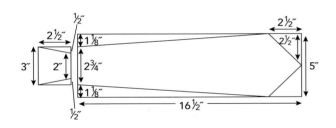

2. Trace the pattern onto fast2fuse.

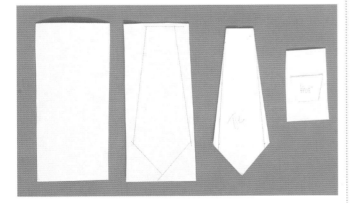

3. Sew the wire to the fast2fuse using a zigzag stitch and white thread. Place the wire as you sew about ¾″ inside the traced outline.

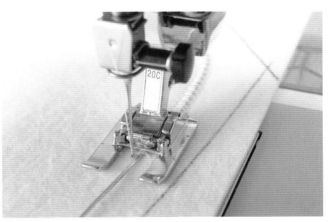

4. Fuse the fabric to the unwired side of the fast2fuse. Cut out the tie.

5. Fuse the other piece of fabric to the wired side of the fast2fuse. Trim the excess fabric.

6. Fuse fabric to both sides of the knot piece. Trim the excess fabric.

7. Satin stitch around both the tie and the knot.

8. With a small straight stitch, sew a ¾″ × 1½″ pleat at the top of the tie. The pleat goes to the back of the tie.

9. Sew the buttons to the back of the tie.

10. Using a glue gun, glue the knot to the top of the tie.

11. With your cord elastic, make a large loop and knot together. Hold the elastic so the knot is in the center. Tie off loops on either side.

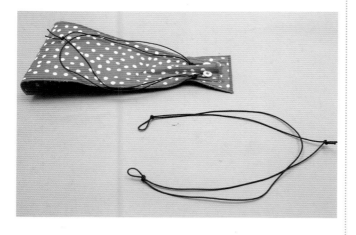

12. Attach the loops around the buttons on the tie, adjusting to fit the wearer's neck. Curl up the tie to suit your fancy.

Variation

The red polka-dot tie is made the same way as the pink one, but without wire in it. The flower is pinned from the back of the tie.

An assortment of eye-popping eyeglasses

silly specs

what you'll need

- A pair of glasses for the base
- 4″ × 8″ piece of prepared fast2fuse
- Matching thread
- Hot glue gun
- Embellishments

How-Tos

Some of the various bases I use to create the spectacular spectacles. I find them at yard sales, thrift shops, dollar stores, and party supply stores.

1. Place the glasses face down on pattern paper. Trace around the outside edges of the glasses. Set the actual glasses aside.

2. Draw an opening inside each traced lens on the glasses pattern. Make sure the opening is large enough to see out of but small enough that the pattern entirely covers the frame of the glasses.

3. Draw the desired shape around the traced lenses onto the glasses pattern. Trace the entire glasses pattern onto prepared fast2fuse and cut out. Satin stitch around the edges.

4. Glue in place on the glasses. I glue one eye at a time so the glue won't dry before I get the pieces in place.

5. Embellish as desired.

For the Star Glasses, I used a pair of costume granny glasses I found at a party supply store. The yellow fast2fuse stars were cut on a die-cut machine. I sewed the stars onto the wire frame by hand.

wings

dragonfly wings

what you'll need

- 26″ × 9″ piece of aqua prepared heavyweight fast2fuse
- 26″ x 6″ piece of heavyweight fast2fuse
- ⅓ yard of pink fabric
- 4″ circle of aqua prepared lightweight fast2fuse
- 2 pieces of 50″ gold cord elastic
- 45″ of 18-gauge wire
- Matching thread
- Hot glue gun

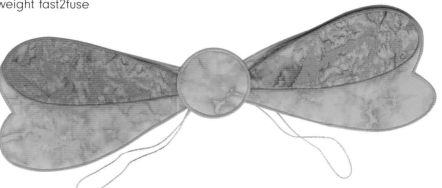

How-Tos

1. Trace the patterns from the pullout onto pattern paper.

2. Trace and cut out the double wing from prepared heavyweight fast2fuse.

3. Trace the single wing pattern onto fast2fuse.

4. Follow the basic steps for adding wire on page 35 to add wire to the single wing. Sew directly onto the fast2fuse with a zigzag stitch. Be careful not to get too close to the edges where you will be satin stitching.

5. Fuse fabric to the unwired side of the fast2fuse. Cut out the wing. Fuse fabric to the other side of the wing. Trim off excess fabric.

6. Satin stitch around all pieces.

7. Refer to the *Butterfly Wings* project (page 39, Steps 6–8) for instructions on attaching the elastic to the wings.

8. Referring to the photo, glue the wings and circle in place.

butterfly wings

what you'll need

- ⅞ yard of heavyweight fast2fuse
- ⅞ yard of lightweight fast2fuse
- 1¾ yards of yellow fabric
- ½ yard of lavender fabric
- ¼ yard each of royal blue, aqua, and purple fabrics
- 2 pieces of 50″ gold cord elastic
- Matching thread
- Angel Dust Ultrafine transparent glitter—Art Institute Glitter
- Fabric glitter glue—Art Institute Glitter
- Foam brush
- Hot glue gun

How-Tos

1. Trace the patterns from the pullout onto pattern paper. (Note that the body pattern is not symmetrical; trace only the half pattern. Trace it onto the fast2fuse, then turn it upside down to trace the other half.) Trace the wing patterns onto heavyweight fast2fuse and cut out. Trace all other pieces onto lightweight fast2fuse. Also cut a 4″ circle from fast2fuse. Cut out the pieces.

2. Fuse the fabrics to one side of the fast2fuse pieces. Trim the edges even with the fast2fuse. Repeat for the other side.

3. Satin stitch around each piece with matching thread.

4. Place the spot pieces to be glittered onto a large piece of copy paper or waxed paper.

5. Paint glue onto the pieces and shake on glitter. Don't worry if you see brush marks in the glue; they'll disappear when the glue dries. Once the pieces are dry, tap off the excess glitter and return it to jar.

6. Treating the 2 pieces of gold cord elastic as one, tie the elastic into a circle. Fold the circle in half with the knot in the center.

7. Carefully pin the elastic to the inside of the wings, about 3″ down from the top center. Try on the wings. Make sure they are snug around the arms and that the tops of the wings are visible above the shoulders. If they are not, adjust the elastic length and placement until you are satisfied.

8. Use your sewing machine and a straight stitch to sew the elastic in place.

9. Use the glue gun to attach the 4″ circle over the stitched elastic. Hold down until the glue is somewhat dry.

10. Referring to the photo, hot glue the various wing decorations and bug body in place.

shoes & feet

silly shoes

I used ribbon to lace up my shoes, but you could use actual shoelaces if you prefer a more authentic look.

what you'll need

- Two 12" × 17" pieces of prepared heavyweight fast2fuse
- Matching thread
- 20 loopy brads—Karen Foster
- Two yards of ¼"-wide ribbon or cording
- Awl or screw punch
- ⅓ yard of ¼" elastic

How-Tos

1. Trace the pattern from the pullout onto pattern paper. Make sure to mark the placement for the laces and elastic on your pattern. Trace onto prepared fast2fuse and cut out.

2. Satin stitch around each piece.

3. Mark each shoe for the hole placement. Drill with a screw punch or make starter hole with an awl. Put the loopy brads in the shoes.

4. Sew the elastic to the shoe heels at the marks on the pattern.

5. Lace ribbon through the eyelets and tie.

Variation

A quick variation to create saddle shoes:

Before Step 3, transfer the shoe "saddle" pattern from the pullout onto fusible web. Apply fusible web onto black fabric. Cut out the saddles and fuse them onto white shoes. Use your sewing machine and black thread to satin stitch around the saddle. Continue with Steps 3–5 as described above.

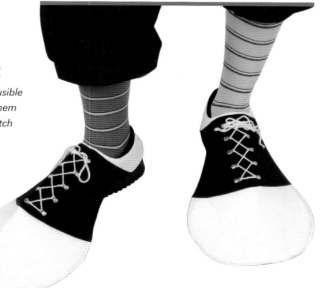

black & white watch

The instructions are for a black and white wristwatch, but a few adjustments and you can make wonderful bracelets, watches, and wrist-bands to match your costume or your little ones' favorite dress-up clothes.

what you'll need

- 1½" × 10" piece of black prepared lightweight fast2fuse
- Two 2" circles of black prepared lightweight fast2fuse
- 1½" circle of white prepared lightweight fast2fuse
- Matching thread
- 1" piece of ¾"-wide black hook-and-loop tape
- 1 black brad—Junkitz
- 2 photo tabs—Junkitz
- Metal numbers—Making Memories
- Hot glue gun

How-Tos

1. Compare wrist measurement to the prepared fast2fuse band. Let the ends overlap about 1". Trim away any excess.

2. Satin stitch around all the pieces.

3. Sew hook-and-loop tape to the ends of the watchband.

4. Join the two 2" circles by placing right sides together. Sew with a straight stitch just inside the satin stitching.

5. Find the center of the watch face and make a small mark with a pencil. Using a screw punch, awl, or large pin, make a hole at the mark. Place the 2 photo tabs over the hole and secure in place with the brad.

6. Center and glue the white watch face to the black circle.

7. Glue the numbers 12, 3, 6, and 9 in place.

8. Try on the watchband and mark where the watch face will fit best. Glue the watch face to the band.

Variations

Make bracelets following the same technique, but instead of attaching a watch face, simply decorate the band with various embellishments, jewels, glitter, paint, broken pieces of jewelry, or whatever strikes your fancy.

These flowery wristband corsages will go perfectly with the Hula costumes (pages 59–61)!

pails 'n' stuff

trick-or-treat pail

These came about because I needed something to put my flowers in. I saw an empty cardboard snack can, and knew I had the perfect base. Once the project was finished, I thought of so many possibilities that I had to share.

what you'll need

- 5¼" × 14½" piece of orange prepared fast2fuse for can
- 1¼" × 14" piece of orange prepared fast2fuse for handle
- Scraps of prepared black fast2fuse
- Snack can
- Orange spray paint
- 2 black ¼" brads
- Matching thread

How-Tos

1. Eat the snacks in the can (my favorite step!).

2. Wash and dry the snack can. Trim the top edge so the can is 5" high all the way around.

3. Spray paint the can orange.

4. Satin stitch around both pieces of prepared orange fast2fuse.

5. With your glue gun, glue the large piece of prepared fast2fuse around the can; you will have about 1" overlap.

6. Cut out 2 eyes, a nose, and a mouth from black prepared fast2fuse. Satin stitch around each piece.

7. Glue the face on the front of the pail.

8. Make a ⅛" hole on each side of the can, 1" from the top edge. Make a ⅛" hole ¾" from each end of the handle.

9. Attach the handle to the pail using the brads.

Variation

This technique was used to create a pirate's spyglass. With an old kaleidoscope (I found one at a thrift shop for 25¢), a little fabric, and a cool skull medallion—you're set!

bouquet of flowers

My personal die-cut machine has some great flower dies, and once again I was off and running! The flowers were just large enough for me to easily stitch around, and small circles were perfect flower centers. These flowers make great gifts for friends. They're perfect for a quick thank-you, or even a "just because" treat.

what you'll need

- 4" × 4" piece of prepared fast2fuse for each flower (in various colors)
- Scrap of prepared fast2fuse for each flower center
- Matching thread
- 9mm chenille stem for each flower
- Screw punch, awl, or sharp scissors
- Hot glue gun

 tip
If you do not have a die-cut machine, try your local scrapbook store to see if you can use theirs, or hand-cut a simple 5- or 6-petal flower! Or use the Hula Girl flower pattern on the pullout.

How-Tos

1. Cut a 3" flower and a ¾"–1½" circle for the flower center.

2. Satin stitch around all the pieces.

3. With the tip of your sharpest scissors, a screw punch, or an awl, make a tiny hole in the center of each of the flowers.

4. From the back of the flower, insert a chenille stem about ½"; bend it over and twist it into a small semicircle. Repeat for all cut flowers.

5. Glue the centers of your flower over the little circle of chenille. Ta-da!

tip
Save time by making a bouquet of flowers at a time! I like to make 5-flower bunches.

Variations

We can all use a little magic once in a while.
Notice the sewing machine button in the center of the wand (Wands, page 32). Add a sewing-themed crown (Crowns, page 24) and there will be no end to the magic you can do!

Here's a special bouquet
for a special teacher. I rolled a wedge of prepared fast2fuse into a cone. I trimmed a scant 2" off the tip so the stems would easily fit into the cone

awards & badges

red, white & blue award

what you'll need

- Two 3″ × 3″ pieces of blue star print prepared lightweight fast2fuse
- 3″ × 3″ piece of white prepared lightweight fast2fuse
- 2″ × 2″ piece of red prepared lightweight fast2fuse
- 4″ × 4″ piece of red prepared lightweight fast2fuse
- Personal die-cut machine (If you don't have one available, see if you can use one at your local scrapbook store, or simply cut out the circles by hand!)
- Star-shaped button
- Matching thread
- Hot glue gun
- Large embroidery needle

How-Tos

1. With your die-cut machine, cut out 2 blue 2¾″ circles, a white 1⅞″ circle, and a red 1¼″ circle. Trace the ribbon pattern from the pullout and cut one from prepared red fast2fuse.

2. Satin stitch around each of the pieces.

3. Following the photo as a guide, place the red ribbon between the blue star circles. Sew the circles together using a straight stitch just inside the satin stitching.

4. Using a large embroidery needle for strength, sew the button in the center of the red circle.

5. Refer to the photo and glue the circles in place.

6. Attach a pin back to the back of the award or glue it to an award sash.

tip *The same technique is used for each of the awards. I painted some of the stars gold to match the rest of the awards.*

award sash

Now that you have all your awards made, you need a place to show them all off! Make a simple sash in any color or print to match whatever your theme may be.

what you'll need

- ½ yard lightweight fast2fuse (more or less, depending on the length you need)
- ⅞ yard of fabric
- Matching thread

How-Tos

1. Following the diagram, make a pattern. Pin the pattern on the wearer to see if you need more or less sash. This piece fits most older kids and small women. Add or subtract at the center of the sash if you need to alter the size to avoid adjusting the slanted ends.

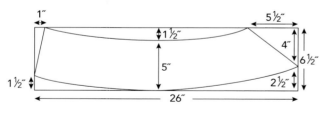

2. Cut 2 sashes from fast2fuse.

3. Fuse fabric to each side of each piece of fast2fuse.

4. Satin stitch around each piece. I went around a couple of times, so the stitching looks very dense and regal.

5. Pin the front of the sash to the back of the sash, overlapping the edges ½″. Place the piece over the wearer's shoulder to adjust the fit. Stitch together the shoulder ends of the sash with a machine straight stitch. Backstitch at the beginning and end of the stitching. Repeat for the seam at the bottom.

tip
When you're making the awards, just die-cut a bunch of various shapes. When you're ready to start making awards, you'll have lots to choose from!

In addition to the standard pin backs, I use various ready-made pins/jewelry as bases for my fast2fuse embellishments.

Variations

With the same technique, you can make wonderful badges or pins to celebrate a hobby or any special occasion.

Because I was having so much fun using my personal die-cut machine, I played around with some other shapes. Circles, hearts, and squares seem to be my favorite and were perfect for awards, pins, and . . . hmmm . . . vary the colors, and they would even make good ornaments for the holiday tree!

bags & purses

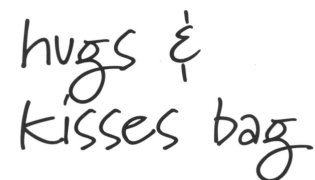

hugs & kisses bag

This bag could be decorated for a variety of occasions with a simple change of color and embellishments.

what you'll need

- 12" × 24" piece of red prepared heavyweight fast2fuse
- 8" × 10" piece of white prepared lightweight fast2fuse
- 6" × 6" piece of black prepared lightweight fast2fuse
- Matching thread
- x and o embellishments—Pressed Petals
- 1¼ yards of 1½"-wide black satin ribbon
- Hot glue gun

How-Tos

1. Trace the patterns from the pullout onto pattern paper. Trace onto prepared fast2fuse and cut out. Cut 2 each of the large heart and the wings.

2. Satin stitch around each piece.

3. Sew the large hearts together using a straight stitch. Start and stop just where the heart starts to curve at the top. Leave the top of the heart purse open so you can keep all your love letters inside.

4. Sew the ribbon in place as a shoulder strap.

5. Using the photo as your guide, glue the additional hearts and embellishments to the front of the purse.

> *I got the heart shape from a die cut. I wanted it to be large enough for the purse so I enlarged it on a copy machine. I made a few different-sized hearts, with the largest being about 12" across at its widest point.*

bling bling purse

A little purse can be tied in with the Bling Bling accessories (page 52) for a very special little girl! I used leopard print; you can use whatever fabric your special girl prefers.

what you'll need

- 3½" × 14½" piece of prepared lightweight fast2fuse
- 6" × 13" piece of fabric
- Two 2" hearts of prepared lightweight fast2fuse
- Matching thread
- ¾ yard of ½"-wide satin ribbon
- Gold circular paper clip
- Small piece of ¼"-wide satin ribbon
- 1 yard of 1"-wide satin ribbon to tie around purse
- Cardboard snack can
- Spray paint to match fabric

Optional Items

- 3 unfinished 1" wood ball feet
- Coordinating acrylic paint and foam brush

How-Tos

1. Wash and dry the snack can. Trim the top edge so the can measures 4" high. Spray paint the can and set aside to dry.

2. Wrap the fast2fuse rectangle around the snack can to ensure a proper fit. Trim off any excess.

3. Satin stitch around the fast2fuse pieces.

4. With right sides together, sew the short ends of the 6" × 13" piece of fabric together with a ½" seam.

5. Turn one edge under 1" and press. Stitch ¾" away from the fold to form a casing. Leave a small opening for the ribbon. Thread the ribbon through the casing.

6. Turn the fabric tube right side out. Slip about 1" of the unfinished edge of the fabric tube over the can. It should be a snug fit.

7. Glue the fabric tube and the fast2fuse rectangle to the can using your hot glue gun.

8. Insert a small loop of ¼"-wide satin ribbon between the 2 fast2fuse hearts and glue them together with hot glue. Loop the heart on the purse ribbon with the gold clip.

Optional: Paint the wooden ball feet with acrylic paint and foam brush. Set aside to dry. Glue the ball feet to the bottom of the purse.

9. Wrap the wide satin ribbon around the purse and tie into a bow. Put a tiny drop of hot glue behind the bow to keep it in place.

capes & medallions

vampire cape

I used cotton for the collar, and satin for the cape.

what you'll need

- 10″ × 22″ piece of black prepared fast2fuse
- 1¼ yards of black satin fabric for cape
- ⅛ yard of black fabric (cotton or satin) for cape ties
- Matching thread

How-Tos

1. Trace the collar pattern from the pullout onto pattern paper. Trace onto black prepared fast2fuse and cut out.

2. Satin stitch around the collar.

3. Trim off the selvages from the black satin. Make a ½″ hem along each edge. (I folded mine twice so the raw edges wouldn't show.)

4. Finish off the bottom of the cape with a 3″ hem.

5. With your machine set to a long straight stitch, sew 2 rows of gathering stitches along the top edge, one ¼″ from the edge and the other ⅝″ from the edge. Pull the threads to gather the fabric, creating pleats and fullness in the cape.

6. Pin the wrong side of the cape to the bottom inside edge of the collar.

7. Sew the cape to the collar using a ¾″ seam.

8. Hold the collar so the cape falls below it. Lightly press the gathers down. Stitch on the edge of the collar to hold the cape in place and enclose the raw edges.

9. Cut 1 strip 3″ wide × the width of the black fabric. Press the lengthwise edges to the center, then fold the strip in half, enclosing the raw edges. Stitch along the edges.

10. Sew the ends to the sides of the collar. See picture for detail. You can leave the tie whole or cut it in half, knotting the ends to finish.

vampire medallion

With this bat medallion, you're set to frighten your friends. To keep a cape in place, make a medallion! Pin the medallion to your shirt, and loop the cape ties around it.

What You'll Need

- Two 4″ circles of red prepared heavyweight fast2fuse
- 1¼″ circle of black prepared lightweight fast2fuse
- 5″ × 6″ piece of black prepared lightweight fast2fuse
- White fabric scraps
- Fusible web scraps
- Matching thread
- Pin back or old advertising pin

How-Tos

1. Trace the bat wings pattern from the pullout onto pattern paper and cut out. Trace 2 wings onto the prepared black fast2fuse and cut out.

2. Satin stitch around all the pieces.

3. Apply fusible web to a scrap of white fabric. Cut out 2 tiny triangle teeth and glue them to the black circle.

4. Place the red circles wrong sides together. Straight stitch the circles together.

5. Using the photo as your guide, hot glue the wings and bat head in place.

6. Sew or glue the pin back into place on the back of the medallion, or glue the medallion onto an old advertising pin.

Glittery circles and diamonds, and a royal "jewel" make a stunning medallion.

Variations

By changing cape tops, colors, and types of fabric, you can create a cape that can easily pull a costume together!

Feeling devilish?

Metallic trims *add a regal touch.*

Padded lamé was used for the fairy princess collar.

A Superhero, *ready to save the day (Wrist Wear, page 41)!*

bling bling

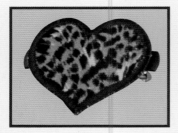

hairclip

what you'll need

○ 2″ heart of prepared lightweight fast2fuse

○ Plain hairclip

○ Hot glue gun

How-Tos

1. Satin stitch around the heart.

2. Hot glue the heart to the hairclip. Hold the pieces together until the glue cools.

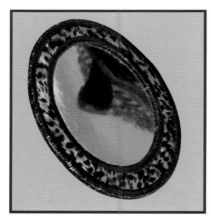

mirror

what you'll need

○ Two 4″ circles of prepared lightweight fast2fuse

○ 3½″ circle of mirror paper

How-Tos

1. Cut a 3″ circle from the center of one of the prepared fast2fuse circles.

2. Satin stitch around both circles.

3. Place the mirror paper face up between the circles.

4. Sew the circles together using a straight stitch just inside the satin stitching.

key ring

what you'll need

- Two 3″-long ovals of prepared lightweight fast2fuse
- Small piece of ¼″-wide satin ribbon
- Gold circular paper clip or plain key ring
- Hot glue gun
- Chipboard letter painted to match fabric
- Tacky glue
- Old keys

How-Tos

1. Satin stitch around the ovals.

2. Insert a small loop of ¼″ satin ribbon between the ovals and glue together with hot glue.

3. Glue the letter to the key ring with tacky glue.

4. Loop the ribbon on the gold clip and add keys.

wrap

what you'll need

- ¼ yard of fabric
- Matching thread

How-Tos

1. Fold about ½″ of both selvage edges to the wrong side of the fabric and stitch.

2. Fold the fabric right sides together lengthwise and sew a ½″ seam.

3. Turn right side out and press.

pirate's hat

With this hat you'll be ready to sail the seven seas!

what you'll need

- 12″ × 20″ piece of black prepared fast2fuse
- 8″ × 10″ piece of heavyweight nonwoven interfacing
- ½ yard piece of black cord elastic
- Matching thread
- Black paint
- Template material

How-Tos

1. Make the headband hat as described in the Headband Hats project (page 23, Steps 1-7).

2. Trace the skull and the crossbones onto template material. Cut out the eyes, nose, and mouth from the template.

3. Trace the skull pattern and crossbones onto the interfacing.

4. Using the skull template as a stencil, dab black acrylic paint through the eyes, nose, and mouth holes onto the interfacing with a foam brush. You may need to go over the area twice to cover it fully. Set aside to dry. Once dry, cut out the skull and bones.

5. Referring to the photo, glue the skull and bones onto the hat.

pirate's eyepatch

what you'll need

- Scrap of black prepared fast2fuse
- Matching thread
- Black ¼" elastic (enough to fit around wearer's head)

How-Tos

1. Cut a rectangle 2½" × 3" from the prepared fase2fuse. Trim the corners for a rounded shape.

2. Satin stitch around the piece.

3. Sew a length of ¼" black elastic to the inside of one side of the patch. Try it on to see how long you'll need to make the elastic.

4. Trim the elastic to the desired length and sew it to the other side of the patch.

pirate's sash

what you'll need

- ¼ to ⅜ yard red fabric

How-Tos

1. Fold the long sides of the fabric together. Lightly press.

2. Trim the ends into a tapering point, starting about 5" in from each end.

3. Fold in half lengthwise and sew using a ½" seam and leaving a 3" opening in the center.

4. Turn right side out and press. Hand stitch or machine sew the opening closed.

 If you need a longer sash, use ½ yard of fabric cut into 2 pieces 9" wide. Sew the short ends together, then follow the How-Tos above.

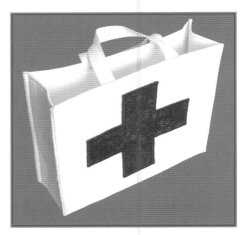

nurse's bag

Here is a fun basic little bag with accessories for your little nurse to keep nursing supplies in one place.

what you'll need

- 26″ × 19″ piece of white prepared heavyweight fast2fuse
- 7″ × 7″ piece of red prepared lightweight fast2fuse
- Matching thread
- ½ yard of white twill tape

How-Tos

1. Following the diagram below, make the bag pattern.

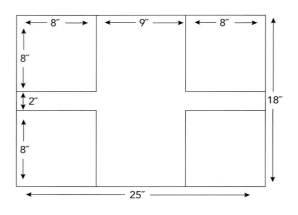

2. Trace the pattern onto white prepared fast2fuse and cut out.

3. Make the cross pattern by measuring a square 6″ × 6″. Measure squares 2″ × 2″ in each corner. Trace the pattern onto red prepared fast2fuse and cut out.

4. Satin stitch around each piece.

5. Match a sidepiece of the bag to a front piece along the satin stitching. Sew just inside the satin stitching using a straight stitch. Backstitch at the beginning and end of your stitching to ensure durability. Repeat for the remaining 3 side seams.

6. Cut the twill tape in half for the handles. Pin the ends ½″ inside the bag, about 3″ from the sides, on both the front and back of the bag. Stitch in place.

7. Using your hot glue gun, attach the red cross to the front of the bag.

nurse's cap

Combine this with the Nurse's Bag and Accessories for hours of dress-up fun!

what you'll need

- 8″ × 11″ piece of white prepared heavyweight fast2fuse
- 4″ × 4″ piece of red fabric
- 4″ × 4″ piece of fusible web
- Matching thread
- Angel button—JHB International
- 2 white ½″ buttons
- ½ yard of white cord elastic
- Shank remover
- Hot glue gun

How-Tos

1. Make the headband as described in the Headband Hats project (page 23, Steps 1–7).

2. Make a cross pattern by measuring a square 3″ × 3″ on the fusible web. Mark a square 1″ × 1″ in each corner.

3. Apply the fusible web to the wrong side of the red fabric.

4. Cut out the cross and fuse it to the front of the cap. If desired, you can stitch around the cross with a zigzag stitch.

5. Remove the shank from the angel button and glue it to the red cross.

name badge

what you'll need

- 2¾″ heart of white prepared heavyweight fast2fuse
- 2 ovals, 2¾″ long, of red prepared heavyweight fast2fuse of red prepared heavyweight fast2fuse
- Matching thread
- Medical-themed button
- Letter brads—Provo Craft
- Pin back
- Hot glue gun

How-Tos

1. Satin stitch around each piece.

2. Join the ovals by placing the wrong sides together and sewing with a straight stitch just inside the satin stitching.

3. Using the photo as your guide, attach brads and buttons to the heart.

4. Glue the heart to the oval base and attach the pin back.

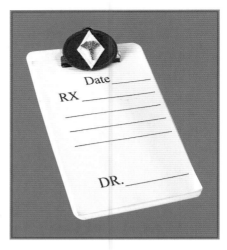

Small clipboard

To complete the look, I included a small nurse's notepad I printed on the computer. For an added touch, tie a pen onto the clipboard using a short length of ribbon.

What You'll Need

- 2 ovals, 3" long, of red prepared fast2fuse of red prepared fast2fuse
- 1¼" diamond of white prepared lightweight fast2fuse
- Matching thread
- Small clipboard
- White acrylic paint and foam brush
- Medical-themed button
- Hot glue gun
- Shank remover

How-Tos

1. Paint the clipboard white (mine took a couple of coats for even coverage). Set aside to dry.

2. Satin stitch around each piece of prepared fast2fuse.

3. Join the ovals by placing the wrong sides together and sewing with a straight stitch just inside the satin stitching.

4. Cut the button shank off with a shank remover.

5. Using the photo as a guide, glue the pieces and button to the clipboard.

hula girls

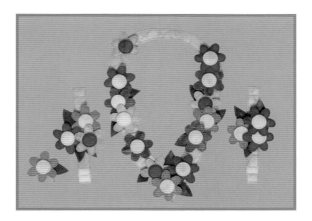

hula girl lei

what you'll need

- 20 squares 3½″ × 3½″ of prepared lightweight fast2fuse in assorted flower colors
- Scraps of prepared yellow fast2fuse for flower centers
- 15″ × 17″ piece of green prepared lightweight fast2fuse
- 3″ piece of hook-and-loop tape
- Matching thread

How-Tos

1. Trace the patterns from the pullout onto pattern paper. Pin together and try on the lei so you can make any adjustment necessary at this point.

2. Cut the lei pieces from the prepared green fast2fuse.

3. Satin stitch around the pieces.

4. Overlap the left ends about ½″ and sew in place. Add hook-and-loop tape to the other ends so you'll be able to put on and take off the lei easily.

5. Trace the flower pattern or use a personal die-cut machine with a 3″ flower and 1⅜″ circle. Cut lots

of flowers and centers from assorted colors. I have 13 flowers on the lei, and I made extras for the hair and wrist pieces. Finish the edges with a tight zigzag stitch.

> **tip**
>
> *I made my leaves from scraps of green prepared fast2fuse—just simple rounded triangles. Finish leaf edges with a tight zigzag stitch.*

6. Referring to the photo, glue the flowers and leaves in place on the lei, making sure not to glue the hook-and-loop tape shut!

hula girl hairclip

I hot-glued a fast2fuse flower and two leaves to a simple hairclip.

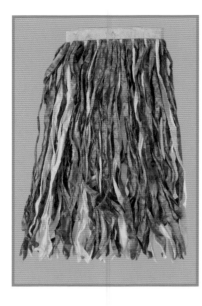

hula girl skirt

what you'll need

- 2½″ wide × waist measurement + 3″ of prepared heavyweight fast2fuse
- 3½ yards total of coordinating green fabrics
- 4″ piece of hook-and-loop tape
- Matching thread

How-Tos

1. Adjust the waistband to the proper length.

2. Satin stitch around the waistband piece.

3. Measure for the desired skirt length. Using that measurement + 1″ as the length, tear the fabric into 1½″-wide strips.

4. Pin the ends of the torn strips onto the inside of the waistband, about ¾″ from the bottom and about 1″ from one end.

 tip *I didn't care if the strips were flat when I pinned them down; in fact, I often bunched up the strips so I could fit them closer together for a really full skirt.*

5. Sew the pinned strips to the waistband with a straight stitch. You can add a second or third row of stitches if desired to ensure that the "grass" strips stay in place.

tip *You could sew the torn strips as you go, but by pinning the strips to the waistband first you have the opportunity to make any adjustments without having to use the seam ripper!*

6. Sew the hook-and-loop tape to the waistband so it is secure.

7. Trim strips as necessary for proper length.

When I started this book, I had a vision of how this costume was supposed to look. I am happy to report it turned out exactly as I pictured it—I love it when that happens!

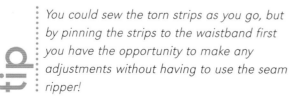

little hula girl lei

You have only the front portion of the lei pattern from the pullout because I chose to close this piece with ribbons. Kids grow so fast! I wanted this lei to be able to handle a growth spurt and be suitable for kids of any age. I also used smaller 2¼″ flowers to keep the same proportion.

Construction is essentially the same, except that, instead of adding the back lei piece to the front, add 1 yard of ribbon folded in half (trim to length needed) on each side.

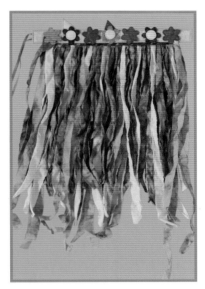

little hula girl skirt

what you'll need

○ 1½″ × waist measurement + 3″ of prepared heavyweight fast2fuse

○ 1½ yards total of coordinating green fabrics

○ 2″ piece of hook-and-loop tape

○ Matching thread

How-Tos

1. Adjust the waistband size. I left mine a bit longer so the skirt would be able to grow as the kid does—for a while, anyway.

2. Satin stitch around the waistband piece.

3. Measure the child from waist to ankle for the skirt length. Using that measurement less 1″ as the length, tear the fabric into 1″-wide strips.

4. Refer to the Hula Girl Skirt project (page 60, Steps 4–7) for making the skirt.

 tip

The skirt will continue to grow with the child if you leave a little space between strips . . . as the child gets taller, you can add a row of longer strips over the first.

cupid's bow

No one will be able to resist the power of love that Cupid inflicts with his little bow and arrows!

what you'll need

- ¼ yard of red fabric
- Matching thread
- 2 yards of black waxed linen thread
- 2″ × 30″ piece of bender board (found at any home improvement store)

How-Tos

1. Cut 1 strip 5″ wide × the width of the red fabric. Sew the strip in half lengthwise, right sides together, to create a tube.

2. Turn the tube right side out and slide the bender board inside.

3. Tie knots in the red fabric at both ends of the bender board.

4. Tie one end of the waxed linen thread to one end of the bow. Make the knot close to the bender board, and tie it tight.

5. Repeat for the other end of the bow, pulling slightly to create a curve in the bender board and pulling the waxed linen thread taut. Tie a tight knot.

cupid's quiver

what you'll need

- 8½″ × 10″ piece of red prepared lightweight fast2fuse
- 3″ x 9″ piece of white prepared lightweight fast2fuse
- ¼ yard of black fabric
- Matching thread
- Tall, skinny snack can
- Black spray paint
- 1″ to 1½″ curtain ring (found at a craft or hardware store)
- Swivel hook (found at a craft or hardware store)
- Hot glue gun

How-Tos

1. Wash and dry the snack can. Trim the top edge so the can measures 8½″ high. Spray paint the inside of the can and set aside to dry.

2. Wrap the fast2fuse rectangle around the can to ensure a proper fit. Trim off any excess.

3. Trace the heart pattern piece from the pullout onto pattern paper. Trace onto prepared fast2fuse and cut out.

4. Satin stitch around all the pieces.

5. With your glue gun, glue the rectangle to the can. Glue the fabric to the can in sections. If you try to cover the can with glue all at once, the glue will be dry by the time you pick up the fabric to place it on the can. Glue the hearts to the front.

6. Sew the curtain ring to the can 1″ from the top.

7. Cut 2 strips 2½″ wide × the width of the black fabric for the strap. Join the ends and trim to 54″ long. Fold the strip in half lengthwise and sew with a ¼″ seam. Turn right side out and fold in ½″ on one end. Press. Slide the swivel hook onto the strap. Tuck the unfinished end into the folded end and sew in place.

8. Hook the swivel hook onto the curtain ring.

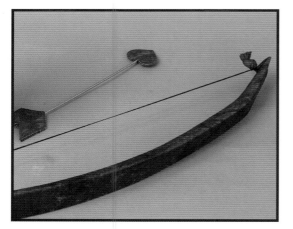

cupid's arrows

what you'll need

- 6″ × 18″ piece of red prepared lightweight fast2fuse
- Matching thread
- Bamboo skewers
- Gold acrylic paint
- Foam brush

tip

Mirror images . . . it can be tricky to have two pieces of satin-stitched fast2fuse match exactly when you've cut the pieces by hand. To make it a bit easier, cut out the first piece as you would any pattern piece, then lay the first cut-out piece right side up on the prepared fast2fuse and trace around it to create your second pattern piece. Mark the right side of each pattern piece with a pin. Satin stitch each piece with the pin side up, so when you put the pieces together, any irregularities in your cutting will match up when you glue them together.

How-Tos

1. Paint bamboo skewers gold with a foam brush and set aside to dry.

2. Trace the patterns from the pullout onto pattern paper. Trace onto prepared fast2fuse and cut out 2 each for each arrow.

3. Satin stitch around the pieces.

4. Using the photo as a guide, glue the remaining hearts and fletchings (arrow tails) to opposite ends of the skewers.

tip

I found it easiest to glue one heart to the skewer, then glue the second heart to the first so you can match up all the edges. Do the same with the fletchings.

shield

I got my idea for the shield by looking up heraldry online. I found some great ideas and some explanations of colors and symbols that helped me make my final color and symbol selection.

what you'll need

- 15″ × 17″ piece of gray prepared heavyweight fast2fuse
- 6″ × 13″ piece of white prepared lightweight fast2fuse
- 10″ × 10″ piece of red prepared lightweight fast2fuse
- Matching thread
- Hot glue gun

> **tip** *Consider using an initial instead of (or in addition to) the crown. There are lots of super alphabet patterns, or use your word processing program to select a font you like and enlarge the letter on a copy machine to get the size you need.*

How-Tos

1. Trace the shield and crown patterns from the pullout onto pattern paper. Trace the shield piece onto gray prepared fast2fuse and cut out. Cut a piece 2″ × 5″ for a handle, also. Trace the crown piece onto red prepared fast2fuse. Also cut three 1¾″ circles. From the white prepared fast2fuse, cut a piece 2¾″ × 11½″ and 2 pieces 2¾″ × 5¼″ for the cross.

2. Satin stitch around all the pieces.

3. Sew the ends of the handle to the back of the shield. Place in the center about 3″ from the top. Stitch a couple of rows so it will be able to handle a battle.

4. Glue the cross in place with the long piece placed vertically and the short pieces placed on either side. This will minimize extra bulk.

5. Using a hot glue gun, glue the crown and circles to the front of the shield.

> **tip** *Create a crown for this knight following the Crown technique (page 24), and he'll be ready to guard the castle!*

Sword

what you'll need

○ 4″ × 17″ piece of silver prepared heavyweight fast2fuse

○ 2 pieces 10″ × 9″ of dark gray prepared heavyweight fast2fuse

○ Matching thread

○ Hot glue gun

How-Tos

1. Following the diagram, make the pattern. Trace onto prepared fast2fuse and cut a blade and 2 handle pieces.

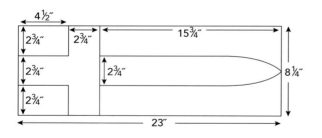

2. Satin stitch around each piece.

3. Place the end of the sword blade between the handle pieces and sew with a straight stitch across the handle pieces.

4. Sew or hot glue the rest of the handle together.

tip

I did not stiffen my sword for safety reasons. You could, however, add a length of wire to the base if you wanted to better control the "bendability" of your sword. Read through the How-Tos on page 35 for adding wire.

elephant

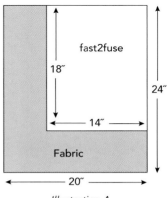

elephant ears

The versatility of fast2fuse made creating an elephant easy!

what you'll need

- ⅝ yard of lightweight fast2fuse
- 1½ yards of gray fabric
- 3″ × 6″ piece of gray prepared lightweight fast2fuse
- Matching thread
- 1 yard of ½″-wide ribbon

How-Tos

1. Cut 2 pieces 18″ × 14″ of lightweight fast2fuse. Cut 4 pieces 20″ × 24″ of gray fabric.

2. Fuse a gray fabric piece to a fast2fuse piece as shown in Illustration A below. Fuse a second piece of fabric on top. Repeat for the other ear, making a mirror image of the first.

 tip *If you want to use different fabrics for the inside and outside of the ears, make sure you cut a left and a right ear.*

3. Cut away the upper portion of each ear. Satin stitch the cut edges. Carefully cut away the lower portion of each ear as shown in Illustration B.

 tip *The fabric ear pieces are larger than the fast2fuse, so you will get a more realistic elephant ear.*

fast2fuse

18″

24″

14″

Fabric

20″

Illustration A

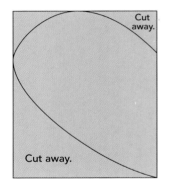

Cut away.

Cut away.

Illustration B

4. Pin to keep the fabric pieces together and satin stitch the remaining edges. Don't worry if the fabric curls; this just adds to the realism and character of the ears.

5. As shown in Illustration C, make 3 darts in each ear. These are tapered darts that are ½" at their widest point.

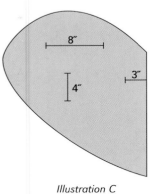

Illustration C

6. Satin stitch around the 3" × 6" piece of prepared fast2fuse.

7. Set the strip on your head and position each ear on the strip and pin. Sew in place.

8. For placement of the ties, try on the ears. Mark a single point on the fast2fuse strip at the back of the jawline on each side of your face. Attach the ties.

elephant trunk

what you'll need

○ 12" × 28" piece of gray prepared heavy-weight fast2fuse

○ Matching thread

○ Two ½" buttons

○ 18" of cord elastic

How-Tos

1. Trace the pattern from the pullout onto pattern paper. Trace onto prepared fast2fuse and cut out. Also cut a piece 2" × 10½".

2. Satin stitch around each piece.

3. Place the trunk pieces wrong sides together. Starting at the tip, sew the top edges together using a straight stitch just inside the satin stitching.

4. Sew the 2" × 10½" piece to the trunk pieces. Start at the tip and straight stitch as before. Remember to backstitch at the beginning and the end of your stitching.

5. Sew a button to each side of the inside of the top of the trunk. Make elastic loops as shown on page 23.

bug

make a bug!

Add to the fun by making several of these creepy crawlers!

How-Tos

1. Cut a 1″ circle and a 2½″ circle of black prepared lightweight fast2fuse.

2. Satin stitch around both circles.

3. Glue the smaller circle overlapping halfway onto the larger circle.

4. For legs, take 3 pipe cleaners (9mm) and twist them together in the center. Place the bug wrong side up and glue the pipe cleaners in place. When the glue cools, bend the legs as desired.

last minute costume

Baseball caps, the un-costume! You've seen those T-shirts that say "This is my costume"? Well, here's a hat with the same goal in mind. Make a small pin as described on page 45, add it to the front of an inexpensive baseball cap, and voila! You have a costume, a gift, or just another way to show off your creativity.

sources

Art Institute Glitter
Amazing color selection of fine glitter, glues for paper and fabric, and a specialty-applicator-tips tool pack

712 N. Balboa St.
Cottonwood, AZ 86326
www.artinstituteglitter.com

Artistic Wire
Permanent-colored copper wire and silver-plated wire, available in more than 50 colors and 14 gauges

752 N. Larch Ave.
Elmhurst, IL 60126
www.artisticwire.com

Beacon Adhesives
Fabri-Tac craft glue, **Hold the Foam** Styrofoam glue, and more

125 MacQuesten Parkway South
Mount Vernon, NY 10550
914.699.3405
www.beaconcreates.com

Blumenthal Lansing Co.
La Mode buttons—decorative and themed button packs

1929 Main St.
Lansing, IA 52151
563.538.4211
www.buttonsplus.com

Cousin Corporation
A full-line bead supplier with a huge selection of beads and beading supplies

PO Box 2939
Largo, FL 33779
800.366.2687
www.cousin.com

Crafter's Pick
The Ultimate! adhesive, usable as liquid glue or contact cement

520 Cleveland Ave.
Albany, CA 94710
510.526.7616
www.crafterspick.com

Darice Inc.
A full selection of crafting supplies, from jewelry findings to foam products

13000 Darice Parkway
Park 82
Strongsville, OH 44149
866.4.DARICE (866.432.7423)
www.darice.com

Dill Buttons
Button manufacturer, maker of the sewing-themed buttons

50 Choate Circle
Montoursville, PA 17754
888.460.7555
www.dill-buttons.com

Ellison
Die-cutting machines and decorative dies

25862 Commercentre Dr.
Lake Forest, CA 92630
800.253.2238
www.ellison.com

EZ Quilting by Wrights
Template plastics in a variety of sizes and styles

Wrights
West Warren, MA 01092
877.597.4448
www.ezquilt.com

Heidi Grace
Heart-topped straight pins and other wondrous papers and embellishments

301 West Main
Auburn, WA 98001
866.89.HEIDI (866.894.3434)
www.heidigrace.com

JHB International
Buttons, buckles, jewelry findings, and more

1955 S. Quince St.
Denver, CO 80231
303.751.8100
www.buttons.com

Junkitz
Various metal embellishments including brads and photo tabs

17 Sweetmans Lane
Building 12
Manalapan, NJ 07726
732.792.1108
www.junkitz.com

K&Company
Cool scrapbook embellishments, including pearl brads

11125 N.W. Ambassador Drive, Suite 200
Kansas City, MO 64153
888.244.2083
www.kandcompany.com

Karen Foster
Scrapbooking embellishment, charms, license plates, rhinestone brads, loopy brads that are great crossovers for decorating costumes.

623 North 1250 West
Centerville, UT 84014
801.451.9779
www.karenfosterdesigns.com

Making Memories
Great metal embellishments including letters, numbers, brads, and photo tabs

1168 West 500 North
Centerville, UT 84014
801.294.0430
www.makingmemories.com

Pressed Petals
A source for your pressed flower and scrapbooking needs.

47 S. Main St.
Richfield, UT 84701
800.748.4656
www.pressedpetals.com

Provo Craft
Art Accents alphabet brads and more

151 East 3450 North
Spanish Fork, UT 84660
800.937.7686
www.provocraft.com

Sizzix
Die-cutting machines and decorative dies

25862 Commercentre Dr.
Lake Forest, CA 92630
877.355.4766
www.sizzix.com

Timeless Treasures Fabrics
Wonderful batik and novelty-print fabrics

483 Broadway
New York, NY 10013
212.226.1400
www.ttfabrics.com

Westrim Crafts
Jewelry findings, beads, charms, papers, tools, kits, and more

Creativity Inc.
7855 Hayvenhurst Ave.
Van Nuys, CA 91409
800.727.2727
www.westrimcrafts.com

about the author

Photo by Gregory Case

Sue Astroth was born in Southern California, where she lived until moving to Concord, California, in 1997. Sue has been a crafter her whole life—needle arts, quilting, and paper arts are her ongoing favorites. Most recently, she has been combining fabric and paper in unexpected ways, demonstrated in her books *Spectacular Cards* and *Make Spectacular Books*.

In 2005 she was fortunate to appear on the *2005 CHA Craft Special* with Carol Duvall and *Simply Quilts* with Alex Anderson, where she demonstrated her first book, *Fast, Fun & Easy Scrapbook Quilts*.

When she isn't in the studio creating new projects, Sue is out collecting treasures for her cards and quilts, pruning the roses in her garden, or working at a local stamp, art, and scrapbook store, where she gets lots of great ideas.

Sue doesn't look back . . . except to say thank you to her family and friends for the love and support she constantly receives along her artistic journey.

great titles from

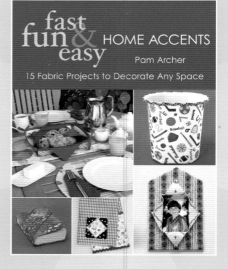

fast fun & easy HOME ACCENTS
Pam Archer
15 Fabric Projects to Decorate Any Space

fast fun & easy FABRIC FLOWERS
Karen Flamme
Beautiful Blooms in an Afternoon

fast fun & easy CHRISTMAS STOCKINGS
Susan S. Terry
Festive Fabric Projects to Stir Your Imagination

fast fun & easy CHRISTMAS DECORATIONS
Linda Johansen
Festive Fabric Keepsakes to Create & Embellish

fast fun & easy FABRIC POSTCARDS
Franki Kohler
Keepsakes You Can Make & Mail

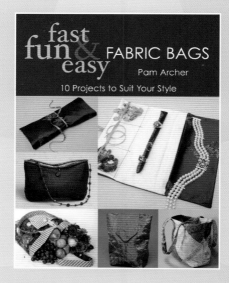

fast fun & easy FABRIC BAGS
Pam Archer
10 Projects to Suit Your Style

C&T PUBLISHING

Available at your local retailer or
www.ctpub.com • 800.284.1114